ADVENT WITH THE ANGELS

A Daily Devotional for Kids

JARED DEES

For more information, visit jareddees.com.

Paperback: ISBN 978-1-954135-04-8
eBook: ISBN 978-1-954135-05-5

First Edition

Contents

The Third Week of Advent

The Fourth Week of Advent

Christmas

Introduction

What do you have at the top of your Christmas tree at home? Most of us place stars or angels at the tops of our trees. Both symbols are reminders of some important Bible stories. The star represents the Star of Bethlehem, which led the wise men to find the infant Jesus. The angel represents the angels who announced the birth of Jesus Christ. Both symbols have one thing in common: they lead us on a journey to the Lord.

Advent is a four-week journey of prayer and preparation for the coming of Christ on Christmas Day. Every journey needs a guide. I invite you to follow the angels as your guide through Advent this year.

On each day of the Advent season, you will pray with the words spoken by the angels in the New Testament. Your goal is to imagine an angel speaking these words directly to you. With each of these words of the angels comes a reflection question, a short meditation, and a simple prayer for the day.

At the end of Advent, you can continue to reflect on the words of the angels on Christmas Day and then throughout the first week of Christmas. There are enough readings and reflections for a full fourth week of Advent, but Christmas Eve and Christmas fall on different days of the week each year. Use as many reflections as there are days of Advent each year, and feel free to revisit the others anytime during the season.

The Advent Angels

If you look around this Advent season, you will start to notice angels are everywhere. They are very popular in Christmas decorations, and we sing about the angels often in our Christmas carols, as well.

Although we can't see the real angels around us today, they are here. Is it any surprise to you that angels are among us as you read this book? Your guardian angel is watching over you, and the many choirs of angels in heaven are singing and praying for you to have a wonderful holiday season.

The angels were with the heroes in the Bible, as well. They played an important role, announcing the birth of Jesus to the world. The Archangel

Gabriel visited the Virgin Mary, Mother of God, to announce the coming of her Son. It was this same angel who came to visit Zechariah, the father of John the Baptist. It may have even been Gabriel who visited Joseph in a dream before and after the birth of Jesus. Then other angels visited the shepherds in the field to announce the birth of Christ and invite them to come and see him for themselves.

The words of the angels included in this book are drawn from these four appearances of angels in the New Testament. To help you understand these words a little better, here is a brief summary of each story:

The Angel Gabriel Appeared to Zechariah

Zechariah was worshipping God as a priest in the Temple when the Angel Gabriel appeared to him. The angel said his wife would have a son, John the Baptist, who would prepare God's people for the Lord. Zechariah doubted the angel's words because he and his wife were too old to have children, but months later the angel's prophecy came true. Zechariah and Elizabeth became the parents of John the Baptist, an important figure during the season of Advent.

The Angel Gabriel Appeared to Mary

The Angel Gabriel appeared to the Virgin Mary. He told her she would become the Mother of God!

She was surprised, since she was not yet married to Joseph, but the angel explained that the Holy Spirit would come upon her so that her child would be the Son of God.

An Angel Appeared to Joseph

Meanwhile, Joseph was visited by an angel in a dream. The angel assured him that he should get married to Mary even though her child was not his own son. After Jesus was born, the angel appeared to him again and told him to protect Mary and Jesus by taking them to live in Egypt for a short time.

Angels Appeared to the Shepherds in the Field

When Jesus was born, God sent a group of angels out to some shepherds in a field. The angels brought good news about Jesus's birth and invited them to meet the Son of God for themselves. They said he would be found wrapped in swaddling clothes and lying in a manger.

The Message of the Messengers

The word *angel* means "messenger." The angels were messengers from God. As you read the words of the angels in this book, you will start to see some common themes in the messages that the angels brought to Zechariah, Mary, Joseph, and the shepherds.

Here are some of the themes you will encounter as you reflect on the words of the angels:

Do not be afraid.

This is the one constant message from almost every angel in the Bible. They all tell the people they visit not to be afraid.

As you journey through Advent and prepare for Christmas, let your fears fade. Listen to the angels. Let God replace your fear with hope and peace.

The birth of Jesus is good news.

Sometimes the Advent and Christmas seasons can be stressful. There is a lot to do! The words of the angels remind us that the birth of Jesus Christ is good news. The birth of Jesus leads to our salvation. As the holiday stress comes upon us, remember that Jesus is with us.

Jesus is the greatest gift.

The first thing most kids think about during Christmas is presents! Gift-giving is a great way for us to remember the greatest gift God has ever given to us: his one and only Son, Jesus Christ. Jesus is the reason for the season. He is the reason we give and receive gifts. Let the angels remind you that any gift we have is also a gift from God.

Listen to the Angels

Christmas is an exciting time! We get to celebrate with all those wonderful Christmas traditions. We get to receive such great presents. As you reflect on the words of the angels these next four weeks, remember where they are leading you.

Follow the angels on a journey toward Jesus. Let your excitement for presents be joined with an excitement for the presence of God.

The First Week of Advent

The First Sunday of Advent

> "Do not be afraid, for your prayer has been heard."
>
> Luke 1:13

What fears can you offer up in prayer?

God gives us a great gift: when we are afraid, he allows us to turn to him in prayer. When you feel worried about anything in life, you can give it to God in prayer. Keep this in mind today. Anytime you feel worried or afraid, say a little prayer to God in your mind. The God who loves you will hear your prayers.

Lord, thank you for hearing my prayers when I am afraid or worried.

Monday of the First Week of Advent

> “You will name him John.”
>
> Luke 1:13

What are the greatest gifts God has given to you?

The name *John* means “God is gracious” or “graced by God.” *Grace* is a word that means “gift.” Through grace, God gives us the gift of his presence. Grace lets us know God is with us. In other words, John the Baptist was given the gift of God’s presence. What a fitting name for Advent as we prepare for Christmas. May we all become little “Johns” and seek the best gifts God has in store for us this Christmas.

Lord, thank you for all the gifts you have given to me in my life.

Tuesday of the First Week of Advent

> "You will have joy and gladness, and many will rejoice at his birth."
>
> Luke 1:14

When was the last time you saw a newborn baby?

Newborn babies bring such great joy into the world. Parents feel the joy. Siblings and grandparents, aunts and uncles feel the joy. The birth of John the Baptist was unexpected. His parents didn't think they could have kids, and when he was born, the family rejoiced. John's parents knew what many others didn't know yet. John the Baptist was no ordinary baby. John the Baptist would bring additional joy and gladness into the world because he would lead people to the one true source of joy: Jesus Christ.

Lord, fill me with the joy and gladness of a newborn baby.

Wednesday of the First Week of Advent

"For he will be great in the sight of the Lord."

Luke 1:15

What makes someone great?

All of us have dreams of being great at something. Athletes dream of becoming all-stars. Writers dream of writing a bestselling book. Actors want to become famous. These dreams are based on what other people think of us. But John the Baptist was great in the sight of the Lord, not people. That should be our goal, too. Let God see your greatness. Don't worry about what other people think about how great or not great you are.

Lord, give me the desire to be great in your eyes and no one else's.

Thursday of the First Week of Advent

"He must never drink wine or strong drink."

Luke 1:15

What are your favorite treats?

Chocolate, ice cream, candy, and treats of any kind can be addicting. It's almost impossible to say no to them. The same goes for wine and strong drinks for adults. It can be hard to say no. But John the Baptist lived a life of saying no to all temptations. He lived most of his adult life in the desert with very little food and no special treats. During this season of Advent and Christmas, when we are surrounded by treats of all kinds, don't forget how John the Baptist prepared to meet Jesus. He said no to treats, and that strengthened his ability to resist temptations to sin. Anytime you say a little no, like to a candy temptation, it strengthens your resistance to sin.

Lord, give me the strength to resist all temptations.

Friday of the First Week of Advent

"Even before his birth he will be filled with the Holy Spirit."

Luke 1:15

What is your earliest memory as a child?

John the Baptist was filled with the Holy Spirit even before he was born. That means he had the Holy Spirit with him during his whole childhood. When you were baptized, you were given an outpouring of the Holy Spirit as well. That means that the Holy Spirit was with you during your earliest memories after your birth and baptism. In each and every memory you have, the Holy Spirit was with you. He remains with you today and will continue to be with you the rest of your life.

Lord, continue to fill up my heart with the love of the Holy Spirit.

Saturday of the First Week of Advent

> "He will turn many of the people of Israel to the Lord their God."
>
> Luke 1:16

Who helps you get to know God?

John the Baptist helped people get to know their God. God loves us all unconditionally, but it is so easy to forget this. We need people in our lives like John the Baptist to point us back to the Lord. Think of all the amazing people that lead us to our God: parents, grandparents, family, friends, teachers, and more. What a blessing they are to us!

Lord, thank you for putting people in my life to turn me toward you.

The Second Week of Advent

The Second Sunday of Advent

> “With the spirit and power of Elijah he will go before him.”
>
> Luke 1:17

Who can you lead to the Lord during this Advent season?

Elijah was one of the greatest prophets in the Old Testament. Many people believed that Elijah would return to Earth from heaven before the coming of the Messiah. Instead, the angel explains that the spirit and power of Elijah will be with John as he goes before Jesus Christ the Messiah. Imagine having this same spirit and power today as you prepare for Christmas. Like Elijah and John the Baptist, God will give us the power to lead others to the Lord.

Lord, bless me with the spirit of Elijah and John the Baptist as I prepare for your coming on Christmas.

Monday of the Second Week of Advent

"He will turn the hearts of parents to their children."

Luke 1:17

How do your parents show you they love you?

Christmastime can be filled with so many joyful family traditions. You and your parents are probably looking forward to celebrating another Christmas together. Do your best to join in the preparations. Help with Christmas decorations. Help with the cooking and baking. Plan presents together. Christmastime is family time. Enjoy it!

Lord, thank you for giving me parents and family members who love me.

Tuesday of the Second Week of Advent

> “He will turn the disobedient to the wisdom of the righteous.”
>
> Luke 1:17

In what ways have you been disobedient lately?

John the Baptist had a simple message as an adult: turn away from sin and ask for God’s forgiveness. To sin is to disobey God. When we ask for forgiveness, we do not need to feel bad about ourselves. The love of God shows us the wisdom of doing the right thing. God’s love shows us why we should be better and gives us the strength to overcome temptation.

Lord, help me to see the wisdom of doing the right thing.

Wednesday of the Second Week of Advent

"He will make ready a people prepared for the Lord."

Luke 1:17

How can you make yourself ready for the Lord's coming on Christmas?

Advent is a season of preparation. We may feel all the excitement of Christmas, but we have to wait for it to arrive. During the waiting, we have the chance to be a little more prayerful and live with a little more purpose. The gifts we get on Christmas represent the gift of God's grace in our lives. These next few weeks allow us to think about how we are acting and change our behavior so that we may feel worthy of those gifts.

Lord, show me the ways I need to prepare for your coming on Christmas.

Thursday of the Second Week of Advent

> “I am Gabriel. I stand in the presence of God.”
>
> Luke 1:19

Where do you feel the presence of God the most?

Gabriel is one of the archangels of God, along with Michael and Raphael. When we join Gabriel and all the angels and saints in heaven, we will get to stand eternally in the presence of God, as well. As Christians, we always stand in the presence of God, but it doesn’t always feel that way. For now, we get to have moments in our lives in which we feel the presence of God. This may be at church or in our families or in small moments of prayer. Look for these moments this Advent season.

Lord, bless me with your presence as I stand before you today.

Friday of the Second Week of Advent

“I have been sent to speak to you and to bring you this good news.”

Luke 1:19

What good news can you share with others about Jesus Christ?

The word *angel* means “messenger.” Angels are messengers from God. In the Bible, they brought a message of good news about the salvation of the world. This is the very same good news that Jesus sends us out to share with the world. Think about your favorite Christmas carol. These songs contain good messages that we can share with others as a reminder of what Jesus did for the world.

Lord, inspire me with the words to share the good news about your birth.

Saturday of the Second Week of Advent

> "But now, because you did not believe my words, which will be fulfilled in their time, you will become mute, unable to speak, until the day these things occur."
>
> Luke 1:20

Have you ever had doubts of what God can do?

Zechariah didn't believe what the Angel Gabriel said at first. He had doubts, and he was punished for those doubts until John was born. We all suffer doubts at one time or another in our faith journeys. During these times of doubt, it is best for us to stay silent like Zechariah. Instead of complaining during the doubt, we can spend more of our time and energy listening to God's word in prayer and in the Bible.

Lord, in times of doubt, let me speak less and listen more to you.

The Third Week of Advent

The Third Sunday of Advent

> “Greetings, favored one!”
>
> Luke 1:28

When was the last time you felt blessed?

When the Angel Gabriel came to Mary, he greeted her and called her the “favored one.” These words are echoed at the beginning of the Hail Mary prayer: “Hail Mary, full of grace . . .” God gave Mary a set of very special blessings to be able to bear Jesus as his mother. God also blesses us throughout our days. He favors us and showers us with gifts. It helps to stop every now and then to appreciate the times when we have been blessed by God.

Lord, thank you for the many blessings in my life today.

Monday of the Third Week of Advent

“The Lord is with you.”

Luke 1:28

How do you know the Lord is with you?

God is always with us. Always! But it is easy to forget his presence during the day-to-day activities of our lives. The Lord is with you now, and he will continue to be with you in every moment of today. Remind yourself of this in everything you do today. God is with you while you sleep, eat, walk, play, learn, speak, and think. He is always with you.

Lord, give me a reminder of your presence in my life today.

Tuesday of the Third Week of Advent

"Do not be afraid."

Luke 1:30

What is the worst thing that could happen to you?

We often dream about the good things we want to happen to us. It isn't so often that we try to picture how things might go wrong. It is scary to think about losing someone we love or something bad happening to us. But these words from the Angel Gabriel reassure us not to be afraid of even the worst possible outcome. God is with us. Do not be afraid.

Lord, thank you for giving me comfort when I am afraid.

Wednesday of the Third Week of Advent

“You have found favor with God.”

Luke 1:30

Who are some of your favorite people in the world?

Mary was one of God’s favorite people. You are one of God’s favorite people. God is proud of you. He is amazed by the many things you can do. Our favorite people in the world make us happy. We want to be around them as much as we can. In the same way, God wants to be around you as much as he can. Try to spend a little extra time with him today. He would love for you to join him.

Lord, I know I’m not perfect, but thank you for loving me as exactly who you made me to be.

Thursday of the Third Week of Advent

“And now, you will conceive in your womb and bear a son, and you will name him Jesus.”

Luke 1:31

When was the last time you left out a game or some toys at night so you could play with them again the next day?

Jigsaw puzzles can be a lot of fun, but they take time. We don’t have to finish puzzles all in one sitting. We can save a puzzle and come back to it later. The same goes for toys. We can leave them out and save the game for later. What does this have to do with Jesus? The name *Jesus* means “God saves.” Like an unfinished puzzle, our lives are incomplete without God. He saves us and gives us the chance to finish the puzzle and have great joy.

Lord, thank you for saving me and giving me the chance to find joy in life.

Friday of the Third Week of Advent

"He will be great."

Luke 1:32

What makes Jesus so great?

There are so many things about Jesus's life that make him great. Pick one of those qualities to reflect on. You already know something about who he was and what he did. He was certainly great, but don't take that for granted. Find something about Jesus that gives you a reason for gratitude. These good things strengthen our faith and love for him the more we think about them.

Lord, you are and forever will be great!

Saturday of the Third Week of Advent

> "He will be called the Son of the Most High."
>
> Luke 1:32

What do you like most about your father?

There are things about our dads that make us proud. You might really like the way he makes you laugh or takes care of you. You might like to tell people about what he does for a living. Jesus's Father was God Most High. Most people would brag about a dad like that! Yet Jesus shares his Father with us. Through Baptism, we become the God's children, too. We get to call God our Father.

Lord, thank you for adopting me as your child so that I get to call you Father like the Lord Jesus.

The Fourth Week of Advent

The Fourth Sunday of Advent

> “The Lord God will give to him the throne of his ancestor David.”
>
> Luke 1:32

What would make someone a great king?

In the Old Testament, God chose David to be the king of his people when he was only a shepherd boy. Jesus was born into a very simple family as well. No one expected a boy from Nazareth to become a king. Yet his kingdom extended beyond Israel. His kingdom combined his Father’s kingdom of heaven and David’s kingdom on the earth. Jesus was a shepherd like David, and we are his sheep. Let’s look to him as our leader and follow him wherever he wants us to go.

Lord, you are my king and my God. I will follow you wherever you go.

Monday of the Fourth Week of Advent

> “He will reign over the house of Jacob forever, and of his kingdom there will be no end.”
>
> Luke 1:33

What are some of your responsibilities around the house?

Our parents trust us to take care of certain things around the house. It might be our responsibility to keep our room clean or put our shoes away. As we get older, our parents give us more responsibilities. God the Father gave Jesus the greatest responsibility. Jesus would rule over the entire universe. Every one of us is his responsibility. Therefore, with great confidence, we rely on him to take care of us.

Lord, thank you for taking such great care of me and of all the universe.

Tuesday of the Fourth Week of Advent

“The Holy Spirit will come upon you.”

Luke 1:35

What are some things that motivate you the most?

The Holy Spirit came upon Mary when the Angel Gabriel visited her, but she was also with the apostles when the Holy Spirit came upon them on Pentecost. When we are baptized and confirmed, the Holy Spirit comes upon us as well. The gift of this Spirit moves us and motivates us to become who God wants us to be and do what God wants us to do. Be open to the Spirit of God, which will guide you and inspire you to do great things throughout the day.

Lord, thank you for the great gift of your Holy Spirit in all that I say and do.

Wednesday of the Fourth Week of Advent

> "The power of the Most High will overshadow you."
>
> Luke 1:35

Do you have any favorite spots in the shade during the summertime?

The shade from a tree or building can be a great way to cool off from the hot sun. Even in the wintertime, the snow in shade melts more slowly because the warmth of the sun is blocked. Mary sat in the shade of the power of God. Imagine the calm she must have felt in the Lord's shadow. We get to seek that calmness, as well. Just like the shade on a hot summer day, God can give us peace in the difficulties of our day. Find some time today to be overshadowed by God and forget the difficult things going on in your life.

Lord, thank you for giving me peace when I need it the most.

Thursday of the Fourth Week of Advent

> "Therefore the child to be born will be holy; he will be called Son of God."
>
> Luke 1:35

What makes you holy?

Jesus Christ was holy. He was holy before his birth. He didn't earn the holiness, because holiness is not a reward for good behavior. We don't deserve holiness. Holiness is a gift from God. He gives it to us because of who he is, not what we do. Jesus was holy because he was the beloved Son of God. You are holy because you are loved by God. If you want to be holy, don't try to earn it by being perfect. Instead, accept and return God's great love for you.

Lord, I want to be holy, and I know that holiness only comes with your great love.

Friday of the Fourth Week of Advent

> "For nothing will be impossible with God."
>
> Luke 1:37

What is one thing you wish could happen but think is impossible?

Christmas is a time for miracles. The angel tells us that nothing (yes, nothing!) is impossible with God. Pray for something impossible. It might not happen right away or on the timeline we wish, but do not forget what the angel said. Nothing is impossible. Have faith and turn to God, and wait in joyful hope for the impossible.

Lord, I know you can do the impossible. Increase my faith in you!

Christmas

Christmas Eve

> "She will bear a son, and you are to name him Jesus, for he will save his people from their sins."
>
> Matthew 1:21

How well have you behaved during this Advent season?

We hear a lot about being on the "naughty" or "nice" lists during the Christmas season. Younger kids often work a little harder to get on that "nice" list in order to earn their presents for Christmas. But Jesus didn't come to punish. The name *Jesus* means "God saves." God sent his Son to save sinners. No one is on God's "naughty list."

Lord, thank you for sending your Son to save me from my sins.

Christmas Day

> “To you is born this day in the city of David a Savior, who is the Messiah, the Lord.”
>
> Luke 2:11

What is the best Christmas present you have ever received?

It probably goes without saying, but the greatest present God has given to us is his only Son, Jesus Christ. As the angel said, this gift is given to you. “To *you* is born this day . . .” he says. God had you in mind when he sent his only Son into the world. Before you were even born, God knew you and sent his Son as a gift for you. What a profound gift this is. During this Christmas season, do not forget that Jesus is sent to us as the greatest gift.

Lord, thank you for sending the Lord our Savior to me.

Second Day of Christmas

> "Do not be afraid; for see—I am bringing you good news of great joy for all the people."
>
> Luke 2:10

What is the best thing that happened to you today?

It is fun to tell our parents, friends, or family the best things about our days. It gives us joy to share good news. The angels brought the shepherds good news about the birth of Jesus. Their fear could be replaced with joy. Don't be afraid to share the stories about God and his role in your life that give you joy. This is the good news to share with all people.

Lord, thank you for all the good moments in my life.

Third Day of Christmas

> "This will be a sign for you: you will find a child wrapped in bands of cloth and lying in a manger."
>
> Luke 2:12

What do you imagine the baby Jesus looked like?

The angels gave the shepherds a very clear picture of how they would find the baby Jesus. He would be wrapped in cloth and lying in a manger. Mangers were long boxes or troughs used to feed animals. This must have been shocking to the shepherds. The Savior of the world and Messiah was lying in a feeding trough? Yet this is the simple way in which our Lord entered the world. No matter how many great gifts you have in your house now, remember the simple birth of the Lord.

Lord, thank you for all the great gifts during Christmas, but help me to remember that none of these gifts will make me happier than you can.

Fourth Day of Christmas

> "Glory to God in the highest heaven!"
>
> Luke 2:14

How do you celebrate when you win a game?

The shepherds overheard the angels praising God and singing, "Glory to God!" They gave God glory, not anyone or anything else. When we repeat these words, either in church or when singing Christmas carols, we join with them in praising God. It is a reminder to always give God glory above anything else we could ever do.

Lord, may I always remember to give you glory when I find success.

Fifth Day of Christmas

> “On earth peace among those whom he favors!”
>
> Luke 2:14

Did you get the chance to experience peace during this Christmas season?

Christmas gives us the opportunity to enjoy the gift of peace from God. Be grateful for those moments of calm and quiet. If you haven’t had the chance to appreciate this gift of peace, find a moment today to seek silence. Imagine the peacefulness of that silent night when Jesus was born. We all need to experience the gift of that calm peace every once in a while.

Lord, thank you for the moments of peace in my life.

Sixth Day of Christmas

> “Joseph, son of David, do not be afraid to take Mary as your wife, for the child conceived in her is from the Holy Spirit.”
>
> Matthew 1:20

Who are some of the best dads you know, and what do they do so well?

Joseph took great care of Jesus and of his wife, Mary. He could have walked away from the relationship, knowing that the baby was not his own, but instead he listened to the angel. He rose to the great call of becoming Jesus’s foster father. What a great model for us to follow as we take care of our own families.

Lord, thank you for the dads I can look up to in my life.

Seventh Day of Christmas

> “Get up, take the child and his mother, and flee to Egypt, and remain there until I tell you; for Herod is about to search for the child, to destroy him.”
>
> Matthew 2:13

What was your favorite part about the last trip you took with your family?

For many people, Christmas is a time of traveling to see family or going on vacation. The Holy Family (Joseph, Mary, and Jesus) traveled during their Christmas season, too. It was an unexpected and a long trip, but they did it together. Enjoy your moments of family time in the car, whether it is for a short trip or a long visit. Those are memories you will share for a long time.

Lord, thank you for the trips we get to experience as a family.

Eighth Day of Christmas

> “Get up, take the child and his mother, and go to the land of Israel.”
>
> Matthew 2:20

What is your favorite part about being home?

As the Christmas season comes to an end, we go back to our everyday lives. Parents go back to work. Kids go back to school. It can be hard to get up on that first day back, but it is important. We have lives to live. Just don’t forget what the seasons of Advent and Christmas were all about. Jesus is given to you as a Savior. He will guide and protect you. He will be with you always for all your days.

Lord, be with me in all I think and do and say.

About the Author

Jared Dees is the creator of The Religion Teacher (TheReligionTeacher.com), a popular website that provides practical resources and teaching strategies to religious educators. A respected graduate of the Alliance for Catholic Education (ACE) program at the University of Notre Dame, Dees holds master's degrees in education and theology, both from Notre Dame. He frequently gives keynotes and leads workshops at conferences, church events, and school in-services throughout the year on a variety of topics. He lives near South Bend, Indiana, with his wife and children.

Learn more about Jared's books, speaking events, and other projects at jareddees.com.

Also by Jared Dees

Jared Dees is the author of numerous books, including a short story collection titled *Beatitales: 80 Fables about the Beatitudes for Children*.

Download a collection of these stories at jareddees.com/beatitales.

Books by Jared Dees

31 Days to Becoming a Better Religious Educator

To Heal, Proclaim, and Teach

Praying the Angelus

Christ in the Classroom

Beatitales

Tales of the Ten Commandments

Do Not Be Afraid

Take and Eat

Pray without Ceasing

Take Up Your Cross

Prepare the Way

Made in the USA
Columbia, SC
25 November 2021